# PUNISHMENT & SLAVERY

BY
WILLIAM ANTHONY

**BookLife PUBLISHING**

©2020
BookLife Publishing Ltd.
King's Lynn
Norfolk PE30 4LS

A catalogue record for this book is
available from the British Library.

All facts, statistics, web addresses and URLs in this book were
verified as valid and accurate at time of writing.

No responsibility for any changes to external websites or
references can be accepted by either the author or publisher.

ISBN: 978-1-83927-090-1

Written by:
William Anthony
(with thanks to Shalini Vallepur)

Edited by:
Madeline Tyler

Designed by:
Drue Rintoul

# CONTENTS

WORDS THAT LOOK LIKE THIS ARE EXPLAINED IN THE GLOSSARY ON PAGE 31.

# THE MOVEMENT OF PEOPLE

Look at the world around you. How many trains set off each day? How many cars pass by your house? Throughout time, people have moved around our planet. They have explored, traded and even fought with other people from all over the world. All of this is possible through the movement of people.

Our world never stands still. People have always wanted to explore and move around the planet and will continue to do so for years to come. Countries have borders and the sky is the limit. How does this affect the world? And how does punishment and slavery change the way that people move around?

# WHY MOVE?

People travel for lots of different reasons. People might travel to visit family, go on holiday or find a new home. There are different reasons for why people move around or leave their home country to find a new place to live. These reasons are sometimes called push and pull factors. Think about it this way: what things might push somebody to leave their home, and what things might pull them to a new one and mean it's a better place to live?

## PUSH FACTORS

- LACK OF JOBS
- PERSECUTION
- LACK OF SAFETY
- CRIME
- WAR
- NATURAL DISASTERS

## PULL FACTORS

- MORE JOB OPPORTUNITIES
- FREEDOM FROM PERSECUTION
- SAFETY AND SECURITY
- BETTER EDUCATION OPPORTUNITIES
- BETTER HEALTHCARE
- BEING CLOSER TO FAMILY

## WHO'S WHO?

Migration means movement. There are lots of different words that you might hear to describe the <u>status</u> of people who migrate, and the reasons for why they might move or be forced to move. Here are a few to help you understand.

**ASYLUM SEEKER:** a refugee who has left their home country and has applied for safety, or <u>asylum</u>, in another country

**EMIGRANT:** a person who leaves their home country <u>permanently</u>, for another country

**IMMIGRANT:** a person who comes to live in a new country permanently, usually for work

**PRISONER:** a person who is held in a prison if they are said to have committed a crime

**REFUGEE:** a person who has been forced to leave their home country or an asylum seeker who has been given permission to stay in another country

**SETTLER:** a person who lives in a country permanently and is allowed to stay for as long as they like

**ENSLAVED PERSON:** a person who is owned by and forced to work for another person, with no pay or <u>rights</u>

# PUNISHMENT AND MOVEMENT

Many people are forced into making the choice to move away from their home. Asylum seekers and refugees may have to leave their countries in order to stay safe. Other people have the choice taken away from them altogether. People who have committed a crime may be sent to a different country as a punishment.

**PEOPLE WHO HAVE COMMITTED CRIMES IN THE PAST MAY NOT BE ALLOWED TO MIGRATE TO A NEW COUNTRY.**

People who have immigrated to a new country are at a high risk of being <u>deported</u> back to the country they travelled from if they commit a crime that is serious enough. However, sometimes people are asked to leave a country for lesser, <u>victimless</u> crimes. Some people are even arrested and deported when they haven't committed any crimes at all.

# PENAL COLONIES

The movement of people as a result of crime has happened throughout history. For many years, people could be sent to the other side of the planet as punishment for committing crimes. <u>Convicted</u> criminals, or convicts, could be sent to live in prisons or work in <u>colonial</u> lands all over the world.

THIS PRISON IN AUSTRALIA HELD CONVICTS TRANSPORTED ALL THE WAY FROM BRITAIN.

Countries such as Britain, France and Russia sent convicts to <u>underdeveloped</u> areas that they owned. These were known as penal colonies. By sending convicts so far away from home, it was hoped that prisoners wouldn't try to escape or return home after they finished their <u>sentences</u>. In these penal colonies, prisoners would be made to work without being paid.

PENAL COLONY IN THE ANDAMAN ISLANDS

ANDAMAN ISLANDS

PRISONERS IN PENAL COLONIES MAY HAVE HAD TO GATHER CROPS, BE SERVANTS, MAKE CLOTHES OR BUILD NEW ROADS, AMONG MANY OTHER THINGS.

# THE BRITISH EMPIRE

## WHAT IS AN EMPIRE?

An empire is a group of countries or areas that are led by a ruling country and leader. Usually, the ruling country is very powerful and controls the other countries and areas. There have been many empires throughout history.

THE OTTOMAN EMPIRE IS A FAMOUS EMPIRE FROM HISTORY. IT BEGAN AROUND 1300 AND ENDED IN 1922.

People moved a lot within empires. People from the ruling country usually travelled around the empire. Slavery and punishment were very common reasons for people being forced to move between different countries within an empire.

SHIPS WERE USED TO HELP PEOPLE TRAVEL FROM COUNTRY TO COUNTRY WITHIN AN EMPIRE.

# THE BRITISH EMPIRE

The biggest empire was the British Empire. British sailors and explorers travelled all over the world and found new places that Europeans had never explored before. Britain began to <u>claim</u> different lands as early as the 1500s.

NEW WORLD

OLD WORLD

THE BRITISH EMPIRE USED PARTS OF NORTH AMERICA AND AUSTRALIA AS PENAL COLONIES.

Some of these new lands that Britain explored and colonised were North and South America. They called the Americas the 'New World', while Europe, Asia and Africa were called the 'Old World'. Settlements, or colonies, of the British Empire were areas of land outside of Britain where people made communities, and these were important to growing empires. Penal colonies were areas like settlements, but set up to take in convicted criminals.

# BRITAIN, NORTH AMERICA AND
# AUSTRALIA

## BRITISH PRISONERS

For much of the 18th, 19th and 20th centuries, Britain used parts of its empire as penal colonies. It deported convicted criminals to places all over the world, including parts of North America, Australia and India.

**BRITAIN STARTED SENDING CRIMINALS TO PENAL COLONIES AS PUNISHMENT IN 1718.**

**THE 1776 UNITED STATES DECLARATION OF INDEPENDENCE ANNOUNCED THAT THE 13 NORTH AMERICAN BRITISH COLONIES WOULD NO LONGER BE OWNED BY BRITAIN.**

## NORTH AMERICA

Between 1718 and 1775, Britain sent thousands of convicts to its penal colonies in America (before it became the United States). As punishment for committing crimes, convicts were sent to America and sold to landowners as indentured servants. Indentured servants were people who signed a contract that said they must work for someone for free over many years. In America, many indentured servants worked on plantations - areas of land where crops such as coffee and sugar were grown. Britain continued to send criminals to America until 1775. One year later, the American colonies fought for <u>independence</u> from Britain.

# AUSTRALIA

After the American colonies declared independence in 1776, Britain stopped sending prisoners there. Instead, it began sending prisoners to Australia. Norfolk Island is thought to be one of the first penal colonies in Australia. British criminals who were moved there were made to grow and gather crops and send them to Sydney, in <u>mainland</u> Australia. However, this didn't work as the crops did not survive the journey.

NORFOLK ISLAND TODAY

In 1803, convicts were moved to Van Diemen's Land. Today, this island is known as Tasmania. This island was closer to the mainland of Australia, so it did not have the problems that Norfolk Island had. Van Diemen's Land was the main penal colony in Australia until 1853. During their time there, convicts would work for free for people who lived there, or in <u>chain gangs</u> that worked on building things such as roads.

AUSTRALIA

TRANSPORTING PRISONERS TO BRITISH PENAL COLONIES ENDED IN 1868, WHEN THE LAST PRISON SHIP TRAVELLED TO AUSTRALIA.

NORFOLK ISLAND

VAN DIEMEN'S LAND

# FRANCE AND RUSSIA

## GLOBAL EMPIRES

The British Empire may have been the largest, but it was not the only empire in the world. France, Russia, Spain and Portugal are just a few countries who each controlled an empire. Each of these empires also set up their own penal colonies all over the world.

DEVIL'S ISLAND

## FRANCE

The French Empire sent many of its criminals to penal settlements as far away as South America and Australia. Devil's Island was France's main penal colony from 1852 until 1953. The prison on the small island was opened on orders from Emperor Napoleon III. The colony was known for being a brutal and dangerous place to be.

## NO WAY OUT

Most of the prisoners sent to Devil's Island were never able to make it back home. Around 70,000 prisoners were sent to the island as punishment, but it is thought that only around 2,000 ever made it back home. Those who tried to escape would have to battle with cruel guards before meeting the sharks that circled the island. Devil's Island was not a place you wanted to be moved to.

SHARKS CIRCLED THE ISLAND WAITING FOR FOOD.

FRANCE ALSO STARTED SENDING THOUSANDS OF PRISONERS TO A PENAL ISLAND CALLED NEW CALEDONIA IN THE 19TH CENTURY.

# RUSSIA

Starting in the late 17$^{th}$ century, the Russian Empire (and the Soviet Union that came later) used Siberia as a penal colony. Siberia is very remote and has a harsh climate, which made life hard for prisoners. Convicts would be forced to work in forests and mines or even build roads and railways across Siberia.

SIBERIA IN WINTER

# MAPPING THE COLONIES

For centuries, punishment has been a huge reason for the movement of people all over our planet. This map shows just how far people were transported across the world.

GIBRALTAR

BERMUDA

BRITISH AMERICA

PUERTO RICO AND CUBA

NORTH AFRICA

FRENCH GUIANA

SPANISH AMERICA

ANGOLA

BRAZIL

- ■ BRITISH EMPIRE
- □ FRENCH EMPIRE
- ■ PORTUGUESE EMPIRE
- ■ SPANISH EMPIRE

**THE LARGER THE CIRCLE, THE MORE PRISONERS WERE SENT.**

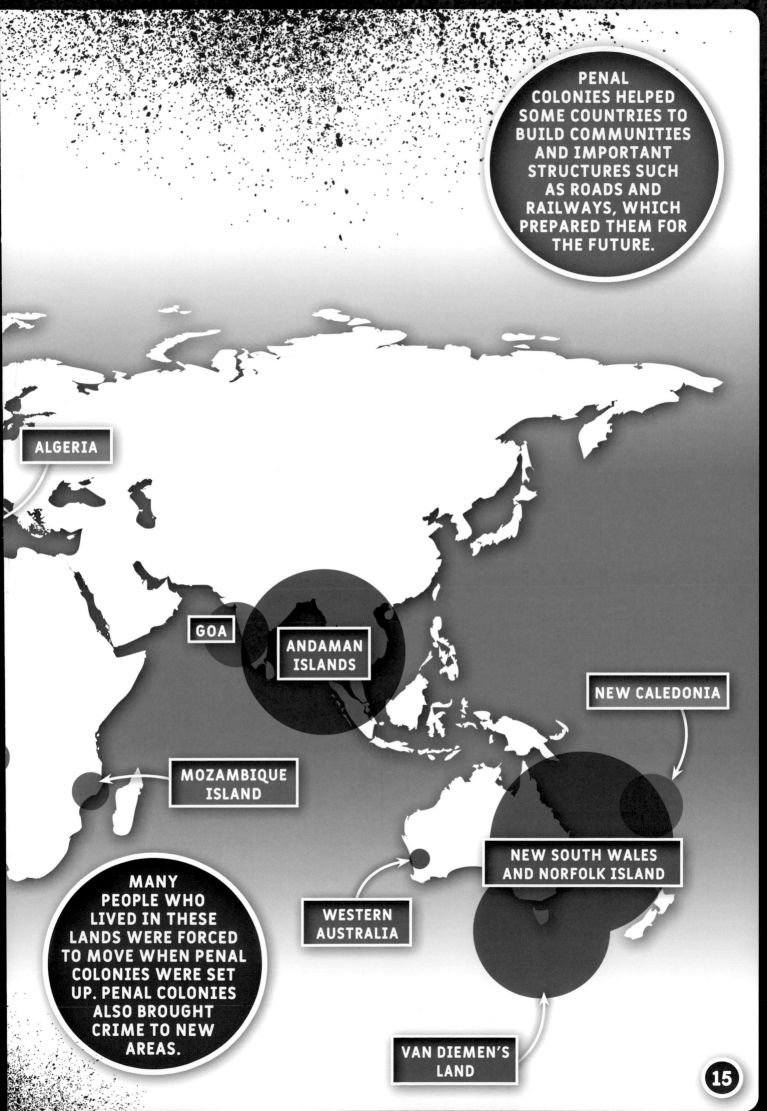

PENAL COLONIES HELPED SOME COUNTRIES TO BUILD COMMUNITIES AND IMPORTANT STRUCTURES SUCH AS ROADS AND RAILWAYS, WHICH PREPARED THEM FOR THE FUTURE.

ALGERIA

GOA

ANDAMAN ISLANDS

NEW CALEDONIA

MOZAMBIQUE ISLAND

NEW SOUTH WALES AND NORFOLK ISLAND

MANY PEOPLE WHO LIVED IN THESE LANDS WERE FORCED TO MOVE WHEN PENAL COLONIES WERE SET UP. PENAL COLONIES ALSO BROUGHT CRIME TO NEW AREAS.

WESTERN AUSTRALIA

VAN DIEMEN'S LAND

# PUNISHMENT AND MOVEMENT
# TODAY

While penal colonies are mostly a thing of the past, crime and punishment still has an effect on the movement of people today. Committing a crime can affect where you can and can't travel, whether you are allowed to stay in a country or not and much more.

IN THE US, IF CRIMES SUCH AS STEALING ARE DETAILED ON YOUR CRIMINAL RECORD, YOU MAY NOT BE ALLOWED INTO THE COUNTRY.

## WHAT IS A CRIMINAL RECORD?

If you have admitted to, or have been found guilty of, committing a crime in the past, the crime is logged on something called a criminal record. Some countries will check your criminal record before you are allowed to visit or move there. These countries will then decide whether or not you should be allowed into the country based on those crimes. People who are not allowed into a country may be sent back to the country they left.

# DEPORTATION

In some countries, people can be deported because of a crime they have committed. The people most at risk of deportation are those who have immigrated to a country and committed a crime, but are not citizens of that country. A citizen is someone who is recognised by law as belonging to a country or area. People can become citizens of a country by either being born there or being given the rights to be a citizen by the government.

**CITIZENS OF A COUNTRY MAY HAVE A PASSPORT FOR THAT PARTICULAR COUNTRY.**

**BEING A CITIZEN NORMALLY MEANS YOU ARE GIVEN CERTAIN RIGHTS, SUCH AS THE RIGHT TO VOTE.**

# THE UK

In the United Kingdom, the Immigration Act of 1971 says that anyone who is not a British citizen can be deported if it keeps the public safe. If a person who is not a British citizen has committed a crime and is sent to prison for more than 12 months, they will be automatically deported from the UK. Sometimes, people can be found guilty of committing a crime that they never actually committed. This means that some people may get deported without ever having committed a crime at all.

**A COURT LIKE THIS ONE WILL DECIDE WHETHER SOMEONE IS GUILTY OF A CRIME OR NOT.**

# SLAVERY

## NO CRIMES AT ALL

The movement of people because of crime was a punishment for the bad things they were said to have done. Many of these people were forced to carry out very difficult work for free. However, many people were forced into the same kind of work without having committed any crimes at all. These people are called enslaved people.

> TODAY, SLAVERY IS ILLEGAL IN EVERY COUNTRY IN THE WORLD. HOWEVER, IT CAN STILL BE FOUND IN SOME PLACES.

IN THE PAST, MANY ENSLAVED AFRICAN PEOPLE WORKED ON PLANTATIONS LIKE THIS.

## WHAT DOES ENSLAVED MEAN?

An enslaved person is owned by somebody else, in the same way that an object or an animal is owned by a person. They have either no rights at all or fewer rights than their owner. A slave owner might want an enslaved person to do work for them, such as manual labour (for example, gathering crops, moving heavy objects and fixing things) or being a <u>housemaid</u>. A slave is expected to do whatever their owner asks them to do.

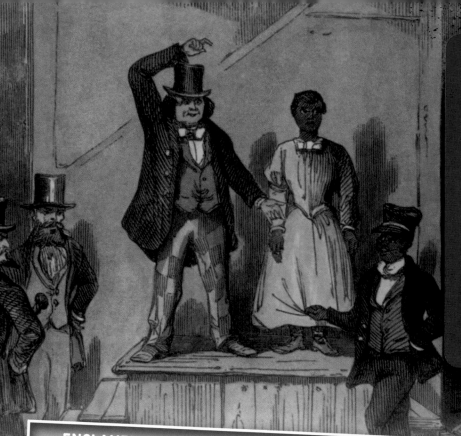

# BUYING AND SELLING

Throughout history, enslaved people have been bought and sold. In the same way you may go to a shop and buy a game or a toy, people came to shops and markets to buy other people. The enslaved people had no choice about being sold into slavery.

ENSLAVED AFRICAN PEOPLE WERE BROUGHT TO MARKETS AND SHOPS, SUCH AS THIS ONE, TO BE SOLD.

# SLAVERY AND THE MOVEMENT OF PEOPLE

Enslaved people can be bought and sold in the same country, but historically many enslaved people were transported across the planet. Big systems were set up in the past to move people around the world so that they could be sold in a different country. The biggest example of this happened between the 15th and 19th centuries and its name was the transatlantic slave trade.

ENSLAVED AFRICAN PEOPLE WERE FORCED ONTO BOATS AND TRANSPORTED ACROSS THE ATLANTIC OCEAN.

# TRANSATLANTIC
# SLAVE TRADE

The transatlantic slave trade was a system of moving enslaved African people around the world in order to make money. It involved three different parts and four different continents – Europe, Africa, North America and South America. This was sometimes known as the triangular trade. This slave trade was responsible for the forced movement of around 12 million African people.

## AFRICA TO NORTH AND SOUTH AMERICA: ENSLAVED PEOPLE

African people were captured either by British traders (people who sold and traded enslaved African people) or by local African tribe leaders. These people were set to become enslaved African people in North and South America. They were packed into ships that sailed across the Atlantic Ocean, on a journey called the middle passage. The ships were overcrowded and dangerous for the African people on board. Of the 12 million African people moved across the Atlantic, it is thought that 2 million people died on the journey.

## NORTH AND SOUTH AMERICA TO EUROPE: MATERIALS

After arriving in the Americas, the enslaved African people were sold. Enslaved people were bought with money or traded for materials such as sugarcane, cotton and tobacco. These materials will have been produced by other enslaved African people already on plantations. These materials were then sent back to Europe for the next part in the triangular trade.

## EUROPE TO AFRICA: PRODUCTS

European countries used the materials sent over from the American continents to make lots of different products. The products made in Europe included cloth, guns, gunpowder and drinks. Some of these products were then shipped to Africa and used as payment for captured African people. In 1700, an enslaved African person would be sold for around £3 worth of products.

# BEING AN ENSLAVED PERSON

The life of an enslaved African person was extremely hard. As soon as an enslaved African person was sold to an owner, they lost most of their human rights and their freedom, had to work extremely hard, obey their owner, and face harsh and brutal punishments every single day.

AFRICAN PEOPLE BEING CAPTURED

## THE JOURNEY

Even before arriving in the Americas to be sold, life was horrible. In the overcrowded ships that sailed the middle passage, enslaved African people were considered objects. They were chained to each other on decks that weren't tall enough for them to stand up. They were not allowed to use a toilet, and when someone died their body may not have been moved for hours. This meant diseases were common on board the ships.

PAINTING OF A SHIP FOR ENSLAVED AFRICAN PEOPLE

THE JOURNEY ACROSS THE MIDDLE PASSAGE TOOK AROUND SIX WEEKS.

# WORK

Enslaved African people had no choice about the work they were given. They had to do whatever their owner asked them to do. Enslaved African people usually worked from sunrise to sunset. Many of them would pick cotton or gather sugarcane and rice from the plantations. Others were told to work inside their owner's home, to wash, cook and clean. In places farther north in North America, enslaved African people may have worked in factories. Even elderly people and children were forced to work.

# PUNISHMENTS

The law did almost nothing to protect enslaved African people. Owners could beat and even kill enslaved people if they wanted to. Punishments for enslaved African people included things such as being whipped, strangled, burned and <u>branded</u>, among many more even worse examples. Enslaved people who gave birth may have had their children taken away from them and sold to other owners.

ENSLAVED AFRICAN PEOPLE WHO REFUSED TO WORK OR ARGUED WITH THEIR OWNERS, EVEN JUST A LITTLE, WOULD BE PUNISHED HEAVILY.

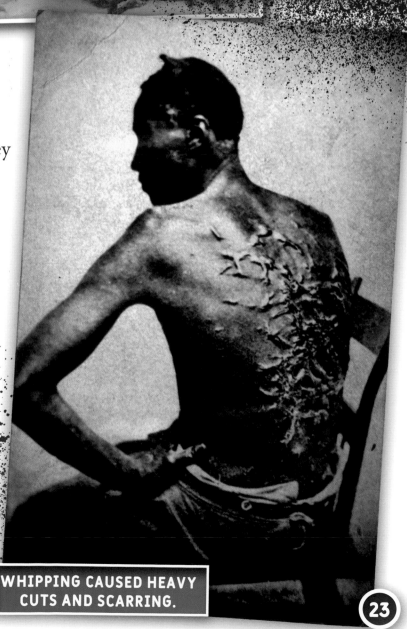

WHIPPING CAUSED HEAVY CUTS AND SCARRING.

# UNDERGROUND RAILROAD

## A WAY OUT

Not everyone in North America supported the slave trade. Some people even helped enslaved African people find a path to freedom. Most of the southern parts of North America supported and took part in the slave trade, but many of the northern parts of the continent did not – these were called free <u>states</u>. Enslaved African people who had escaped their owners in the South would try to travel northwards, using the path to freedom called the underground railroad.

## WORK

The underground railroad was not an actual railroad with trains and tracks, but the system used lots of railway language. Any enslaved African people who had escaped their owners would try to find the nearest <u>safehouse</u> – these were known as 'stations' in the railroad. In each station, there was a 'stationmaster'. These were usually white Americans who would protect and hide people who had escaped from police and owners until it was safe for them to continue their journey north towards the next station.

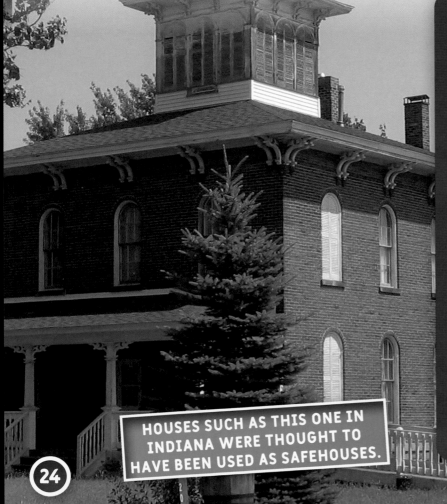

HOUSES SUCH AS THIS ONE IN INDIANA WERE THOUGHT TO HAVE BEEN USED AS SAFEHOUSES.

# RISKS AND LAWS

The path to freedom was full of dangerous risks, even in the free states of the North. The Fugitive Slave Acts of 1793 and 1850 were laws that gave anyone the right to capture enslaved African people who had escaped. The law also said the enslaved people must be returned to the place they escaped from, where it was very likely that they would be brutally punished. Anyone found to be helping enslaved African people to escape would also be punished. This meant that nowhere was completely safe.

ENSLAVED AFRICAN PEOPLE WERE ALWAYS AT RISK OF GETTING CAUGHT BY SLAVE CATCHERS.

CANADA WAS A SAFE PLACE FOR ENSLAVED AFRICAN PEOPLE WHO HAD ESCAPED.

# CANADA

The goal for many enslaved African people was to reach the US border with Canada. Unlike the US at the time, Canada offered Black people the freedom to live where they wanted, respected their human rights and let them be part of the government. Those who moved enslaved African people from station to station on the underground railroad were called 'conductors'. These people were also responsible for helping enslaved African people on the last part of their journey into Canada, where they would finally become free.

AROUND 30,000 TO 40,000 ENSLAVED AFRICAN PEOPLE WERE HELPED TO FREEDOM IN CANADA BY THE UNDERGROUND RAILROAD.

# ABOLITIONIST MOVEMENT

## PROTESTING SLAVERY

It wasn't until the 18th century that people began to truly <u>protest</u> the slave trade. Many religious groups began to <u>criticise</u> the slave trade because it did not respect the rights of every human. By the end of the 18th century, lots of people across the Americas and Europe had turned against slavery.

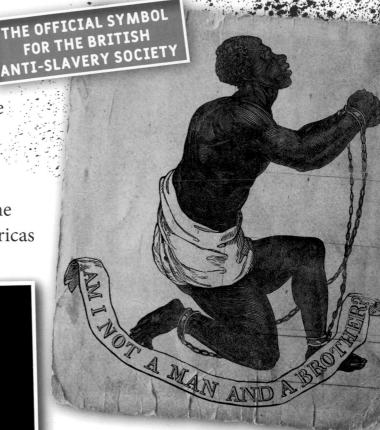

THE OFFICIAL SYMBOL FOR THE BRITISH ANTI-SLAVERY SOCIETY

AM I NOT A MAN AND A BROTHER?

IT TOOK BRITAIN AROUND 20 YEARS TO PASS A LAW TO STOP THE TRADING OF ENSLAVED PEOPLE.

WILLIAM WILBERFORCE

## BRITAIN

British <u>abolitionists</u>, such as William Wilberforce and Thomas Clarkson, achieved a huge victory at the beginning of the 19th century. They believed that the only way to end the suffering of enslaved African people was to ban the transportation of African people through the transatlantic slave trade. Finally, in 1807, The Abolition of the Slave Trade Act made the slave trade within British colonies illegal.

# UNITED STATES

The US also banned the <u>importing</u> of enslaved African people in 1807, but banning slavery altogether was a different task. Many states relied on slavery for money, so trading continued within the US. Throughout the early 1800s, lots of attempts to stop the abolition of slavery took place, including the Fugitive Slave Act of 1850. However, in 1863, President Abraham Lincoln passed the Emancipation Proclamation, which freed all enslaved people in the southern states. Two years later, Lincoln officially abolished slavery in the Thirteenth Amendment to the <u>US Constitution</u>.

**PRESIDENT LINCOLN AT THE FIRST READING OF THE EMANCIPATION PROCLAMATION**

# THE END OF AFRICAN SLAVERY

Criticism around the world towards slavery had grown so strong that, one by one, countries were beginning to abolish it. The last South American countries to practise slavery – Cuba and Brazil, who were trading with Portugal – completely abolished slavery in the late 1880s. As a result, one of the largest systems in history for the movement of people had finally ended.

27

# SLAVERY TODAY

Slavery may have been outlawed in the 19th century, but sadly it still exists in today's world. There aren't any big systems like the transatlantic slave trade; slavery exists in different ways to the past. There are thought to be over 40 million people in slavery around the world.

Modern slavery exists in many different forms. Some of the most common types of slavery are:
- Being forced to work: when people are made to work with the threat of being punished if they don't
- Debt bondage: when people borrow money that they cannot repay and are forced to work to pay off the money they owe
- Child slavery: when children are made to work for someone else's benefit, such as by being soldiers
- Forced marriage: when someone is married without their <u>consent</u> and cannot leave the marriage

Modern slavery is still responsible for the movement of people. Human trafficking is a common form of slavery found all over our planet. It involves people being moved from place to place to be <u>exploited</u> for work. People who are experiencing lots of push factors (check back to page 5) tend to be targeted by human traffickers.

OVER HALF OF THE PEOPLE TRAFFICKED FOR SLAVERY ARE MOVED TO NEW COUNTRIES.

Human traffickers may offer these kinds of people a job and a better life elsewhere, while lending them money to help them pay for the travel. When the person arrives, the job may be dangerous and they may be forced to work for free to pay off their debts. Sometimes, the job may not exist at all, and the person is forced to do something else. Other times, the person may not choose to go somewhere else – they may just be kidnapped. This form of movement through slavery can be within one country or spread across the entire planet.

FACTORS SUCH AS WAR CAN LEAD SOMEONE TO TRY TO FIND A NEW LIFE ELSEWHERE.

# ACTIVITY

Punishment and slavery can be difficult topics to think about. They can be very sad topics and sometimes even a little bit scary. However, it is important to discuss these topics with your friends, family and teachers, no matter how scary they seem. Here are some things you could talk and think about:

How do you think prisoners felt after being moved so far away from their families to the penal colonies around the world?

Can punishment ever go too far? What kinds of punishment are okay and what kinds of punishment are not okay?

How do you think enslaved African people felt when they were being forced to work on the plantations of North and South America?

Why do you think the stationmasters and conductors on the underground railroad put themselves in danger to help enslaved African people escape?

How do you think it felt for the enslaved African people who were lucky enough to reach freedom?

# GLOSSARY

**abolitionists** people who strongly want something to be stopped

**asylum** protection given to somebody by a state or government

**branded** to have had a mark burned into the skin to show who owns the person

**chain gangs** groups of prisoners who are chained together while they do work outside a prison

**claim** to say that something belongs to you

**climate** the usual weather conditions in a particular place

**colonial** of or relating to a colony (a country or area of land owned and ruled by another country)

**consent** agreement or permission for something to happen or be done

**continents** very large areas of land, such as Africa and Europe, that are made up of many countries

**convicted** to have been found guilty of a crime and sent to prison

**criticise** to express disapproval of someone or something

**deported** when somebody has been made to leave a country

**exploited** to have used someone in a way that helps someone else unfairly

**housemaid** a servant who does things such as cleaning and laundry

**importing** bringing a product into a country to be sold

**independence** when an area or country is not ruled by another country and has control of itself

**mainland** the large area of land that forms a country or a continent and does not include islands

**natural disasters** natural events, such as earthquakes or floods, that cause serious damage and loss of life

**permanently** lasting forever

**persecution** cruel or unfair treatment based on religion, political beliefs, where a person is from or what they look like

**protest** show disagreement about something through actions

**remote** far away from other people, houses, cities and more

**rights** things that a person can have or do because of the law

**safehouse** a place where a person hides from authorities, such as the police

**sentences** the punishments given by a court of law

**Soviet Union** a country in eastern Europe and northern Asia that no longer exists, which was made up of Russia and many Asian and eastern European countries

**states** regions of a country that are controlled by the country's government but that have the power to make their own laws about certain things

**status** a person's position and situation at a particular time, to do with moving to new countries

**tribe** a group of people that includes many families and relatives who have the same language, culture and beliefs

**underdeveloped** having a low level of production and a poor standard of living

**US Constitution** a document that holds all the laws by which the United States is governed

**victimless** when nobody is hurt or affected

# INDEX

## PHOTO CREDITS

Images are courtesy of Shutterstock.com, unless stated otherwise. With thanks to Getty Images, Thinkstock Photo and iStockphoto.

4&5 - IGORdeyka. 6&7 - joloei, StaryLyss, Iwelam [CC BY-SA 4.0 (https://creativecommons.org/licenses/by-sa/4.0)], Peter Hermes Furian, Peter Hermes Furian. 8&9 - Peter Hermes Furian, Everett - Art. 10&11 - tonympix. 12&13 - Nick_Nick, Matyas Rehak, wildestanimal, Maksimilian. 14&15 - vectorlight. 16&17 - EQRoy, tuaindeed, Sergey Shik, MR.Yanukit. 18&19 - Sergey Shubin, Everett Historical. 22&23 - Everett Historical, TR STOK. 24&25 - Everett Historical, CC BY-SA 3.0, https://en.wikipedia.org/w/index.php?curid=6029179, David Carillet. 26&27 - sutham, Everett Historical. 28&29 - Anan Kaewkhammul, 271 EAK MOTO, Tomas Davidov. 30 - Gelpi.